DIMENSIONS
OF A
WORSHIPER

DIMENSIONS
OF A
WORSHIPER

Wilmer Estrada Carrasquillo

EDICIONES
GUARDARRAYA

Ediciones Guardarraya
La Antillana Calle B #9
Trujillo Alto, PR 00976

ISBN: 979-8-9875322-6-3

CONTENT

CHAPTERS

THANKS!

Although the author's name appears on the cover of a book, the reality is that writing a book is a work completed thanks to a community of people. Undoubtedly, I had a community that accompanied and helped me throughout the process of writing this book.

First, I want to thank Laura, Kalani, Mía, Valeria, and Anthony. Their patience gave me the space to write and edit the book. They also allowed me to share my thoughts from time to time.

Second, I want to thank our local church, *Comunidad de Esperanza* (Community of Hope), for allowing me to lead a six-week Bible study based on this book. Their questions, comments, and feedback were invaluable.

Third, I would like to thank the team that assisted me in editing and translating the book. Kalani, Anette, and Carolyn, thank you for taking the time to improve the manuscript. Your input improved the final product. Yet, I take full responsibility for any errors.

Fourth, countless people approached me after hearing the sermon titled "The Dimensions of a Worshiper" and encouraged me to turn the sermon into a book. You are the unsung heroes of this book. Your words of encouragement inspired me to begin and complete this book.

Finally, to the One worthy of all glory and honor, God. I hope that every day I can live out what I write in this book.

INTRODUCTION

WE WILL BE MEASURED

Revelation 11.1

The act of measuring comes up several times in the Bible. It is applied in geographical spaces, in structural elements, in church practices, and in the daily life of human activity. Zechariah 2 indicates that when the prophet raised his eyes, he saw a man who was going to measure Jerusalem because he wanted "to find out how wide and how long it is" (Zechariah 2.2). At the end of the book of Revelation, John describes the measurements of the city walls. According to the measurement, the wall was "144 cubits thick" (Revelation 21:17). In the book of

Leviticus, we find instructions on the measurements of offerings, which vary according to the sacrifice and family. For example, one of the offerings was a "handful of the flour and oil" (Leviticus 2:2), as determined by the priest. Lastly, in his letter to the church at Ephesus, Paul instructs them to grow until they attain "the whole measure of the fullness of Christ" (Ephesians 4.13). This one, to make a point of difference, is incalculable. Beyond numbers, this is a way of life.

TEMPLE, ALTAR & WORSHIPERS

In Revelation 11:1, John is given a measuring stick to measure the temple, the altar, and those who worship in it. The relationship between these three elements is interesting. The temple is the place of worship, the house of the Lord. In the Old Testament, the tabernacle was situated in the center of the tribes. When the pillar of cloud and fire came to a stop, the tabernacle would be assembled, and the tribes would arrange themselves around the tabernacle. Once the tabernacle became a temple, it became the center of life for the people of God. Following this pattern, John uses the exact image of the tabernacle when he describes the coming of Jesus to the world. "And made his dwelling among us" (John 1.14). Jesus, as the very presence of God, dwelt in the center of creation.

The altar played an important role in the lives of the people of God. On one hand, the altar was a symbol that reminded them of what God had done on their behalf. On the other hand, the altar represented a place of sacrifice. When Moses received the instructions to build the tabernacle, he also received instructions to build at least two altars, the altar of incense and the altar of burnt offerings. Both altars were integral to the rituals of the Jewish religious system. Even though both are of utmost importance, one of them, the altar of incense, was placed in front of the veil that divided the Holy Place from the Holy of Holies. This is the most intimate space of the tabernacle.

Finally, those who worship in the temple are the people of God united as a community of worship. However, it is essential to recall that, in the Old Testament, only the chosen lineage — the descendants of Aaron and the Levites — were permitted to serve in the tabernacle. Once a year, the high priest was able to go past the veil to present the atoning sacrifice for the people. But thanks to the sacrifice of Jesus, the veil was torn, and now we all have access to it. Today, not only do we have access to temples and altars, but we have also been given access to the very presence of God.

A careful reading of Revelation 11.1 reveals that the verse begins with a broad perspective on worship and then moves to an intimate vision of it. In other words, it moves from the structure of the temple to the personal. The three elements — the temple, the altar, and the worshipers — share a common aspect of worship. This shift from general to intimate is made possible by the death and resurrection of Jesus. The lives of those who have confessed Jesus as their Savior become a temple and a sacrifice. On the one hand, as Paul says, "You yourself are God's temple, and God's Spirit dwells in your midst" (1 Corinthians 3:16-17).

On the other hand, we should offer our "bodies as a living sacrifice" (Romans 12.2).

Bible scholars who have carefully studied Revelation 11.1 agree that the text does not specify how the worshipers are measured. But what is clear is that those who worship in the temple will be measured. Before the silence of how we will be measured, I propose a way forward.

FOUR DIMENSIONS

In the letter that Paul sent to the church in Ephesus, he stated that to comprehend God's love, we need to "grasp how wide and long and high and deep is the love of Christ" (Ephesians 3.18). In this verse, Paul presents four dimensions to help us understand the love of Christ. These dimensions are width, length, depth, and height. Interestingly, these are the basic measurements required to construct a building. Although each dimension is unique, the four measurements are interconnected.

If a structural engineer overlooks the interconnections among these four dimensions, it could result in a catastrophe. A building that fails to consider one of these measurements is not a safe place. Unfortunately, I have seen how buildings that fail to meet construction codes often cannot withstand strong winds, earthquakes, or other natural disasters. For Paul, the totality of God's love can only be experienced when we have fully grasped these four dimensions. Let's take a brief look at the significance of these measurements.

Width is defined as the distance from one side to the other, extending from left to right or vice versa. The width presents itself as the contraposition of length. Length refers to the distance established from the front portion of a structure to the back. The height is the distance between the tallest and lowest portion of the structure. Just like width and length have a relationship, so do height and depth. This last dimension refers to the distance between the surface of the structure and its foundation. All these measurements, working together, produce the basic elements of a safe structure.

Following this idea, I aim to establish that these four dimensions will be measured when assessing individuals who worship in the temple.

The Christian life is not passive. We must keep busy and active in the work of our salvation (Philippians 2.12). Those who worship in the temple will be measured (Revelation 11.1). This is a reality that we cannot deny. I dared to say that John did not speak of a quantitative measurement. Though the quantity is important, it is not the central focus. I want to argue that John refers to a qualitative measurement. In other words, the quality of those who worship. Would that be the reason why Jesus says to the Samaritan woman, in John 4.23, that the Father is looking for worshipers in spirit and in truth? These two qualities point to the attitude of a worshiper and the quality of the worship. Such worshipers are those who live every day, growing in their height, depth, width, and length of their worship.

I hope that the development of these dimensions allows us to enhance our Christian experience. For example, a movie with four dimensions integrates vision, sound, touch, and movement, providing participants with an enjoyable and complete experience. In a certain way, the movie with four dimensions encourages us to move from being spectators to participants. In other words, our whole being would feel what is going on. Maybe this is Paul's reason for discussing the four dimensions of love.

Similarly, Jesus says the following when he summarizes the commandments: "Love the Lord your God with all your heart and with all your soul and with all your mind and with all your strength." (Mark 12.30). Building on the commandments that Moses shared with Israel, Jesus summarizes them in two commandments and follows that summary with four dimensions: heart, soul, strength, and mind. On this occasion, Jesus doesn't use measuring terms; he uses tangible aspects of human life.

FROM SPECTATORS TO PARTICIPANTS

Following this idea, I hope that integrating the words of John in Revelation, the words of Paul in Ephesians, and the words of Jesus in Mark will provide you with an understanding of the argument I am presenting. The experience of worship cannot be a mere invitation to be spectators. On the contrary, it is an invitation to participate with all our being. The spectator only observes, but the participant lives what is happening. Living brings with it a process of growth and maturity.

When Moses told the people of Israel to love the Lord with their whole heart, soul, and strength, it was not only so they could exist, but so they could live. This sense was not lost when Jesus repeated these words in the book of Mark. Jesus did not call the disciples just to exist; he called them so that they could live. In the same form, God did not call the church just to exist; he called it to live. To be in Christ is to live. In the words of John 10.10, "I have come that they may have life, and have it to the full." I dare to

SUCH WORSHIPERS ARE THOSE WHO LIVE EACH DAY EXPANDING THE HEIGHT, DEPTH, WIDTH, AND LENGTH OF THEIR WORSHIP.

say with the same certainty that the basis of all of this is found in Genesis. God did not create humans to exist like mere spectators. God created humans to live, to be participants. He blessed us to live. Because he lives, we can live, and those are the worshipers whom the Father seeks.

Matthew, Luke, and Mark all narrate a story in which Jesus tells his disciples that the moment would come when a stone wouldn't be left upon another. With this phrase, Jesus refers to the temple. Similarly, in His conversation with the Samaritan woman, Jesus reveals to her that the time would come when "you will worship the Father neither on this mountain nor in Jerusalem" (John 4.21). In a way, what Jesus manifests to the Jews (his disciples) and the Gentiles (Samaritans) with these arguments is that locality does not override attitude. The locality rests upon rocks; attitude rests upon the heart. Rocks only exist, but the heart is the engine of life. I believe this is the reason why we see a transition from the law being written on stone (Exodus 34.28) to the law being written on the heart (Romans 2.15 and Hebrews 10.16).

As you read this book, I invite you to keep these questions in mind. Am I only existing, or am I living? Am I existing as a spectator or living as a participant? Am I content with the rigidity of the rocks, or do I desire the flexibility of the heart? I hope, as you move from page to page, you continue to expand your dimension as a worshiper. When we only exist, we will be stuck in what is known as dimension zero. This dimension represents itself as a dot. This dimension is flat; it lacks height, depth, width, and length. In other words, it exists, but it lacks value. That was me at one point, but there is so much more to do in this life. It is my prayer that you may live and walk to the rhythm of God's heart so that you may grow in depth, height, width, and length.

Discussion questions:

1. How do you interpret the concept of being measured as a worshiper in the context of your own faith journey?
2. In what ways can we apply the principle of measurement found in Scripture to our daily lives?
3. How does understanding the relationship between the temple, the altar, and worshipers deepen your appreciation for worship?

DEPTH

distance between the surface
of the structure and its foundation

ONE

DEPTH

Ezekiel 47.5

I was born and raised on the island of Puerto Rico. I lived there until my early thirties. I spent countless hours at the beach enjoying water sports. I quickly learned that there are three basic rules to follow when spending a lot of time in the water. The first is that the more body mass there is outside the water, the more control you have over your body.

In other words, as you walk towards the deep end, you start losing control over your movements. This rule helps you determine if you are maintaining a safe distance from the shore. The second rule is, never trust that what happens at the surface is similar to what happens under the surface. Occasionally, even though the surface may appear calm, there may be undercurrents. These undercurrents run in the opposite direction from the shore, making them very dangerous. This rule teaches you to look before you get in. Sometimes, you can see where underwater currents are. With these first two rules, we have come to the last one. Avoid going into the water by yourself. At a very early age, I learned a saying that goes like this, "The ones who drown are the ones who swim." In other words, the risk of drowning is typically faced by someone who ventures into the water. However, if you go with others, the probability of survival increases. If you are reading this story today, it is a testament to the importance of these rules.

RIVERS FLOW

The biblical text on which this chapter is based is found in the book of Ezekiel. This chapter starts with Ezekiel in the temple. According to the biblical narrative, a man took Ezekiel to the temple for the third time. But on this occasion, Ezekiel sees something that he didn't see the first two times. He goes on to say, "and the water was trickling from the south side" (Ezekiel 47.2). Following the phrasing of the writer, these waters were not stagnant; they were flowing from the south side. The man guiding Ezekiel, similar to the one in Revelation 11.1, had a measuring rod. On this occasion, it was not used to measure the temple, the altar, or those who worship in it. In this story, the measurement will be the expansion of the water that flows from the temple.

Using the rod that he had in his hand, the man "measured off a thousand cubits" (Ezekiel 47.3). Approximately 1,700 feet, or about 530 meters. Ezekiel walked behind the man. When Ezekiel got to the end of the measurement, he noticed something. The water flowing from the temple covered his ankles. But the man did not want Ezekiel to stay there. In verse 4, it states that he measured another thousand cubits. Again, Ezekiel followed. Once he reached the end of the measurement, Ezekiel said he led him through "water that was knee-deep." Until this moment, Ezekiel had full control over his body, as there was more body mass outside the water. However, the guide did not leave him there. The narrative continues, stating that the man took the measuring rod and measured another thousand cubits. Ezekiel followed him, and this time the water reached his waist. With water at this level, we begin to lose control over our bodily movements, as half of our body is submerged. Nevertheless, the man measured another thousand cubits. On this occasion, Ezekiel tells us something that reveals he can no longer stand upright. "The water had risen and was deep enough to swim in –a river that no one could cross." (Ezekiel 47.5). When Ezekiel says that he cannot cross it, he refers to walking. In the first three measurements, he was able to walk. In this one, he couldn't. The only way to cross the river is by swimming it. At this point, Ezekiel is at the mercy of the current. It is so deep that he no longer has control.

THE FRUIT OF THE DEPTH

At the beginning of this chapter, I mentioned that it is not a good idea to be in the water by yourself. Those around us are the ones who can help us in case we are in waters that can only be crossed by swimming. This is what happens in verse 6. The man who guided Ezekiel brought him out and took him to the bank of the river. Not the temple, where everything started. At this point in the story, Ezekiel saw several things that were the product of the expansion of the water. First, "I saw a great number of trees on each side of the river" (Ezekiel 47:7). Second, the river reached the Dead Sea and "the salty water there becomes fresh" (Ezekiel 47:8). Third, wherever the river flows there is an abundance of fish and "everything will live" (Ezekiel 47:9). Fourth, there will be so much abundance that those who fish will throw their nets because of the abundance and variety of fish (Ezekiel 47:10). Fifth, despite the transformative effect of the river, the salt waters of "swamps and marshes" will not be destroyed (Ezekiel 47:11). Sixth, the trees will give fruit. Its leaves will be used for healing. All of this is possible, "because the water from the sanctuary flows to them" (Ezekiel 47.12).

As I mentioned previously, the depth is the distance between the surface and the furthest point from the foundation. I'll explain the definition in more detail to create some connections with the reading of Ezekiel. Every building has a surface. Everything that we see from the building starts from the surface. However, every building must also have a foundation. The distance from the surface to the lowest point of the foundation is one of the key dimensions that contribute to the structure's stability. But unfortunately, that foundation is not seen. The construction of the foundation requires time, investment, and a lot of work, but the work is not appreciated until strong winds, earthquakes, or other disasters may come. The purpose of the foundation is not to make the building look attractive, but to ensure its structural integrity remains intact. In other words, endurance. The depth of the foundation will be associated with the other three dimensions.

Along with the foundation, there is another crucial element that plays a significant role. the landscape. Testing the landscape is crucial for any construction project. It is essential to become familiar with the characteristics of the ground on which you will build and ensure that it is suitable for construction. This test is of utmost importance. It does not matter if the foundation is solid; if the ground on which it is being built is loose or unstable, it is not a good decision. This is why Jesus says that those who build on solid ground are wise. But those who build upon the loose ground are foolish men. Only one of these houses can withstand the storms of life (Matthew 7:24-27). Which one? The one built on solid ground.

WORSHIPERS OF DEPTH

Let's put aside the buildings and houses, and let's think about us. The worshipers will be measured. Therefore, how is your foundation? In other words, how solid is the ground you are building on, and what is the depth of the foundation of your worship? Besides the example I mentioned in Matthew 7, I would like to mention another important example highlighting the importance of building upon solid ground. Every human being worships something. Everyone's heart is fixed on something. This is what the writer says in Proverbs 4.23: "Guard your heart, for everything you do flows from it." Even though we may not like how this sounds, if God is not the one who guides our hearts, something else would be guiding us. When other things guide us, it becomes idolatry. I say this to establish that our dimensions as worshipers should be built on solid ground. There is no ground more solid than Jesus Christ. Our heart should be fixed on him. Following this idea, Peter says, "Jesus is the stone you builders rejected, which has become the cornerstone" (Acts 4.11). Blessed are those who build their foundation on this rock.

Although having Jesus as our cornerstone is sufficient, it does not exempt us from our responsibility as builders. In Matthew 7, Jesus makes clear that the act of building is our responsibility. The development of the dimensions of a worshiper in spirit and truth is in our hands. The Father has given us the cornerstone (Jesus Christ) and the guide (Holy Spirit), but it is our responsibility to build upon solid ground. How can we do it? I'll give you one way to do it.

Let's revisit the story of Ezekiel. The man guiding Ezekiel is described as the angel of God in other versions. In other words, this guide symbolizes God's presence. In this story, there is no one else—just the man guiding Ezekiel and Ezekiel himself. This makes me think that those who want to be truly devoted worshipers should learn how to spend time alone in God's presence. The height, width, and length of a worshiper depend on our ability to have intimate moments with God. This forms the foundation that helps carry us through difficult times, though no one can see it.

The second thing that happens in this story is that Ezekiel does not take a step into the deep without being guided by the man. In other words, Ezekiel gives up his will and follows the man's steps. Once again, this man represents

BUILDING A FOUNDATION TAKES TIME, EFFORT, AND INVESTMENT, BUT IT WON'T BE APPRECIATED UNTIL STORMS OR EARTHQUAKES HIT.

the presence of God. Therefore, a worshiper with depth not only sets time apart with God, but also gives up their will and follows God's steps, even when they are not clear where we are going. When we learn to spend time alone, we learn to follow in his footsteps.

Lastly, we see Ezekiel placing his confidence in the man who was guiding him. To the point that, even when he was losing his step, instead of going back to a level of security, he followed. Even when he needed to swim. A person who desires to be a worshiper with depth should not fear the possibility of losing self-stability. A worshiper in spirit and truth must begin to leave behind the levels of comfort until they encounter the fullness of the presence of the depth of God. David says the following in Psalms 42.7: "Deep calls to deep in the roar of your waterfalls; all your waves and breakers have swept over me." Can you imagine a scene like this? But even there, David felt the Lord's security. David would go on to say in the same chapter, "God is my rock" (v. 9).

It is not my intention to paint a reality that is easy to achieve. Though I still love to go to the beach, I do so with caution. Entering the depths of the ocean is something that may trigger our anxiety. However, amid this challenge, remember that God's presence is guiding us step by step. You may not see the impact of the water that flows out of the temple, but you can still follow the one who is calling you to the depths of the waters. Walk, dig deep into the rock that is Jesus Christ. As you walk, remember the promise of God for his people, "When you pass through the waters, I will be with you; and when you pass through the rivers, they will not sweep over you." (Isaiah 43.2).

Discussion questions:

1. What does having a solid foundation in your faith mean to you, and how do you actively work on it?
2. How can personal experiences, like swimming in deep waters, serve as metaphors for our spiritual growth?
3. In what ways can you develop deeper connections with God and others in your worship practice?

HEIGHT

the distance between the tallest and
lowest portion of the structure

TWO

HEIGHT

Exodus 30.1

The day before I began writing this chapter,
Anthony, our youngest son, was telling me
about something that happened at school. He
was very excited and told me that he had
learned about cold and hot elements. On that
day, they experimented with dry ice. He was
very surprised by two things that he learned.
First, he told me with a very excited tone, "How
is it possible that ice can burn you?" His mind

could not comprehend how something cold could burn you. The second thing that drew his attention was the smoke produced by the dry ice. Anthony told me, "It is dense, and instead of going down, the smoke rises."

I was around the same age when I had a similar experience. There was a specific route in Puerto Rico that caught my attention. This route led us to the west side of the island. There was an area where I could see a tower-like structure that always had a flame. This tower had a wide base, but the highest point was narrower. The scene made it look like a giant candle. Every time we passed by that area, my parents or siblings would tell me, "Wilmer, there is the candle, blow it out!" Of course, I blew and blew many times.

As time went on, I stopped blowing when we passed the candle because I realized that I would never be able to blow it out. My curiosity about this grand candle changed. On the other hand, I began to wonder why it would never turn off. Days would pass, and the fire would still be present, even though it was sometimes difficult to see. The night would come, and the flame would still burn. But something else caught my attention. I started to ask questions about the fire and the smoke. The fire burns upwards, and the smoke rises with it. To satisfy my curiosity, one day, I lit a match and began to move it back and forth on its axis. My experiment confirmed what I had observed from the car: both the fire and the smoke always run upward.

You might wonder why. I am not a pyromaniac, but this is what I've learned. Due to gravity, cold air tends to sink, while warm air rises. This interaction between cold and warm air plays an important role in processes. This phenomenon is called convection, which refers to the transfer of heat through vertical movement. When you light a candle, the convection current pushes the cold air downward because of the heat. Conversely, warm air, being less dense than cold air, rises, causing the flame to point upward. Following this pattern, smoke is produced during combustion. The combustion makes the surrounding air less dense. As a result, the smoke, a product of combustion affected by heat and the minimal density of the fire, rises instead of falling.

THE ALTAR OF INCENSE

I hope I didn't bore you with this story and with the explanation of convection. I think it will make sense as you keep on reading. The biblical story that serves as the foundation for this chapter is found in Exodus 30. Exodus 30 is part of a more extended conversation that God has with Moses about the tabernacle and the worship that is offered in it. Specifically, this chapter explains the instructions given to Moses for the construction of the temple, including the furniture to be used and the people who would serve in it. (The God who is going to measure us is the God who gave the instructions for the temple, the altar, and those who worship in it.) Among the furniture that God asks Moses to build, there are two altars. One of them is the altar of the holocaust. This altar was in the atrium, and on it, they offered the sacrificed animals. The other altar, the one I want to highlight, is the altar of incense. This altar was to be placed inside the tabernacle (Exodus 30.6), and all the furniture inside the tabernacle contributes to the worship experience in the Old Testament.

Chapter 30 begins by stating that Moses would build an altar of incense. The incense is a blend of distinct elements that are crushed together to create a spice, which, when burned, produces a pleasing aroma and dense smoke. This altar has three primary interpretations. First, the incense would overtake the smell that arose from the burnt offerings at the altar of the holocaust. Second, the smoke has been interpreted as a sign of God's presence. Thirdly, the smoke is interpreted as the people's worship, rising before the presence of God. This last one will be the center of this chapter.

Besides building the altar, God gave Moses additional instructions. Verses 7 and 8 state that this altar would burn continually. First, God tells Moses, "Aaron must burn fragrant incense on the altar every morning when he tends the lamps. He must burn incense

KEEP THE FIRE BURNING DAILY, FROM GENERATION TO GENERATION.

again when he lights the lamps at twilight." The instructions specify burning twice a day; it is possible that the amount of incense used in the morning was sufficient to keep the altar lit continuously until evening. On the other hand, the end of verse 8 adds another element of continuity, which states, "Incense will burn regularly before the Lord for generations to come." The first instruction emphasizes the priestly responsibility to maintain the altar of incense. The second discusses the communitarian responsibility to maintain this practice from one generation to the next.

The importance of this altar moves beyond its continuous burning and the preservation of the practice from generation to generation, but also to its placement inside the tabernacle. The altar of incense would be in the holy place, along with the table of showbread and the golden lampstand. But only one of them would be placed next to the veil. Exodus 30.6 says, "Put the altar in front of the curtain that shields the ark of the covenant law — before the atonement cover that is over the tablets of the covenant law — where I will meet with you."

The sanctuary was divided into two sections, the Holy Place and the Holy of Holies. Inside the Holy of Holies, you could find the ark of the covenant. A curtain separated one from the other. Following the instructions, the altar of incense would be placed on the side of the Holy Place, but in front of the ark. The only thing that separated the altar of incense and the ark was the veil. And there, in that place, it would burn daily, twice a day, and from generation to generation. The fire burning the incense kept the worship of the people rising constantly before the presence of God.

If we revisit the conversation about the giant candle and the process of convection, we can recall that what caught my attention was how the flame and smoke remained elevated. Interestingly, the symbol that God uses to represent the prayers of the people is the altar of incense. Both elements that interested me in my childhood are the same ones that are presented now. On this altar, the incense would burn so that the pleasing smell would rise into God's presence. Additionally, this altar, similar to my experience with the giant candle, would burn day and night.

There is another important detail regarding the altar of incense. Previously, I mentioned that the incense was a mixture of elements that were crushed until they were pulverized. This mix had to be pure. In Exodus 30.34-35, this process is detailed for us. "Take fragrant spices — gum resin, onycha and galbanum — and pure frankincense, all in equal amounts, and make a fragrant blend of incense, the work of a perfumer. It is to be salted and pure and sacred." There were no shortcuts in creating the incense. God was clear; he said to Moses, "Do not offer on this altar any other incense" (Exodus 30.9). There was no substitute and no excuse. The elements that were described were the ones to be burned. Can you imagine the responsibility that those in charge face? They were responsible for maintaining a large reserve of incense to prevent depletion.

Maintaining the altar of incense involved lighting it twice daily, along with performing alternating tasks and continuously monitoring to ensure a sufficient supply of incense, preventing any interruption in its burning.

FIRE, INCENSE, AND SMOKE

What do fire, incense, and smoke have to do with being worshipers of height? On one occasion, one of the smoke detectors at my home signaled that the battery was dead. It started to beep when we were sleeping. One of our daughters asked me to disconnect it and not turn it back on again. As you can imagine, I told her no because it is an essential gadget in case of a fire or gas leak. Immediately, I explained the use and the reason for its placement in the highest parts of the house. She asked if we had a water sprinkler fire suppression system in our home. I explained that in our home, we have sensors that activate an alarm but do not release water.

It is not typical to find these types of sensors in a house. This system is more common in commercial or public buildings. The only way these water pipes can be activated is when the sprinkler breaks or melts due to exposure to a specific temperature. Therefore, the sensor can only be activated and send a signal to the water pipe when there is the presence of fire or smoke. Here lies the relationship between fire, incense, smoke, and worshipers of the heights. Water will be released when smoke or fire rises.

WORSHIPERS OF HEIGHT

I hope that the following analogy effectively illustrates my point. A worshiper of height is a person who comes into the presence of God with incense prepared to be burned. If there is smoke lacking, it's not because of a lack of altar or fire. These two elements are present in all moments. On the contrary, the two reasons why the smoke would be lacking are the lack of incense or the worshiper's failure to make it a priority. But when these two are present in the temple, it is possible to burn an aromatic offering in the presence of God. In the event of a gas leak or a building fire, this would activate the smoke sensor and the water pipes. Many buildings are prepared for an event like this. A building that complies with fire codes will have detectors and water pipes installed.

In comparison, when worshipers go to the temple, they should have in mind that God is present, but His manifestation is revealed to us through the smoke that rises from the worship that we present in God's presence. I stated that one way smoke was represented was as a symbol of God's presence. With this, I do not want to imply that the presence of God is limited to the moment when incense is burned. This is an error. God is always present, but when incense is burned, it reveals or manifests that God has been present all along. Let's remember that the temple is the house of God.

The reality is that there are moments when the fire and smoke are so dense that they become indistinguishable. In the same way, even though the smoke produced by the altar of incense and the presence of God have their unique properties, these fuse when we offer our worship. The question that we must ask ourselves is the following: Is water falling? In other words, is the presence of God being manifested? If our answer is no, then we must ask ourselves, are we offering a kind of worship that is pure? It may be that if there is no water falling, or we do not see the manifestation of the presence of God, it is because no smoke or worship is rising in the Holy place.

Discussion questions:

1. How does understanding the concept of height in worship influence your relationship with God?
2. What role does the image of fire play in worship, and how can we cultivate it in our lives?
3. How can we encourage one another to reach new heights in our worship and spiritual practices?

WIDTH

extension of a structure

from one side to the other

THREE

WIDTH

John 12.3

Laura loves board games. If you look around our house, you will see that we have a closet full of them. A few years back, she brought home a giant version of the game known as Jenga. This game consists of players taking turns removing one block at a time from the tower and placing it on top, creating an increasingly unstable structure. This process requires the player to make good decisions and maintain control of their pulse and motor skills. I thought that "if the tower is big, it is more stable." I quickly learned that it was not the case. Even though the blocks were bigger and had the impression of being more solid, the relationship between the height and the width made the game difficult.

At some point in the game, the tower will fall. This is part of the game. The game ends when one of the players causes the tower to fall. The Jenga does not have a foundation, and its width is not proportional to its height. So, the question is not, will it fall? The question is, when will it fall? This question makes sense in a game whose end goal brings excitement to our lives, but it should not be like that when it is about our real lives. Why? Because the result could be disastrous.

Many biblical stories can help us understand what I mean by the width of a worshiper. However, there is one story found in the Gospel narratives that came to mind.

Although there are unique differences in the stories, a common thread unites them. It is the moment when Jesus is anointed by a woman while sitting at the table. Therefore, to provide a clearer and more comprehensive picture, I will refer to the four Gospels: Matthew 26.6-13, Mark 14.3-9, Luke 7.36-50, and John 12.1-10.

AND THE HOUSE WAS FILLED

Jesus was invited to dinner. None of the New Testament narratives mention that the host provided the usual hospitality upon a guest's arrival. According to ancient customs, the host should wash the visitor's feet with water, dry them with a cloth, and offer a kiss. Yet, this did not happen. All four narratives place Jesus reclining at the table with other guests.

While Jesus was at the table, a woman arrived holding a jar of perfume. Matthew, Mark, and Luke do not name her. Matthew and Mark describe her by saying, "a woman came … with an alabaster jar" (Matthew 26.7, Mark 14.3). Luke, on the other hand, adds another descriptor, "a woman … who lived a sinful life"

(Luke 7.37). In John's version, the woman is Mary, Martha, and Lazarus's sister.

According to biblical scholars, this perfume was expensive. None of the authors tells us how the jar of perfume was obtained, but I will share one possibility. One option is that families with daughters stored perfume in a jar to give to their future husbands on their wedding day. Accumulating this perfume was time-consuming because it was costly. However, giving this jar held double significance—both monetary and sacrificial. If this jar symbolizes a family's labor on behalf of their daughter, it lends a profound meaning to the interaction between the woman and Jesus in this event.

Mark and Matthew do not provide a lot of detail; they only say that the woman approached, took the jar of expensive perfume, and anointed Jesus' head. However, the versions of Luke and John reveal some details that help me gain a wider understanding of what I want to present in this chapter. In Luke's and John's accounts, it's the feet of Jesus that are anointed. John describes that while the table is being served, Mary takes the jar of perfume and "poured it on Jesus' feet" (John 12.3). But besides anointing him, Mary makes another gesture. John goes on to describe that Mary, "wiped his feet with her hair" (John 12.3).

Following Luke's narrative, Jesus was already reclined at the table. On this occasion, it is not Mary; Luke describes her as a sinful woman who found out Jesus was at that house. This woman also arrived with an alabaster jar of perfume. When she saw him, Luke describes that "she began to wet his feet with her tears. Then she wiped them with her hair, kissed them and poured perfume on them" (Luke 7.38). As we can see in Luke, before anointing his feet with perfume, the woman cleanses Jesus' feet with her tears, wipes them with her hair, and then kisses them. In other words, the woman offered the customary hospitality that the host had neglected to provide before anointing him.

Her act of worship did not go unnoticed. On the contrary, they provoke different reactions from those present. The writers reveal that Simon the Pharisee, Judas Iscariot, the disciples, and others were present. Their reactions were very similar. All of them stated that the woman's action was a waste and suggested it would have been better to sell the perfume and donate the proceeds to the poor.

In response, Jesus confronts all those present at the dinner. And in all four accounts, he lets them know that what she had done was in preparation for his burial.

UNEXPECTED HOSPITALITY

Why am I presenting this story as an example of width? I will bring together a few responses from each account. Firstly, Simon (Luke) dared to question Jesus' identity because a sinful woman was touching him. "If this man were a prophet, he would know who is touching him and what kind of woman she is — that she is a sinner." (Luke 7.39). However, Simon's ego prevented him from seeing that the same thing could be thought about Jesus, being in his house. Furthermore, the presence of this woman revealed Simon's heart, as he failed to offer hospitality to Jesus.

In second place, Simon is so focused on himself that he cannot recognize that a woman who does not live in his house and was not invited is a better host than he is. As a result, Jesus confronts Simon and makes it clear that, as the host and the one who had invited Jesus, he had not received him correctly. "You did not give me any water for my feet... You did not give me a kiss... You did not put oil on my head" (Luke 7.44-46). However, this woman offered what the host could not.

Third, the negative reaction from those who did not understand what was happening at that moment did not diminish the impact of the woman's actions on Jesus. Among the four accounts, John mentions an incident involving perfume. That's why this chapter begins by referencing John 12.3. John states at the end of the verse, "and the house was filled with the fragrance of the perfume" (John 12.3). This phrase strikes me as very significant. For John, it's such an important detail that he includes it

THE BREAKING OF THIS JAR HAD A DOUBLE VALUE, THAT IS, FINANCIAL AND EMOTIONAL.

in his story. Jesus was not the only one who benefited from the perfume – John and everyone in the house did too.

Finally, the stories found in Matthew and Mark declare a testimony that we still remember today. According to Matthew and Mark, her actions went beyond the four walls of the house. Jesus, addressing those who are in this house, adds, "Truly I tell you, wherever this gospel is preached throughout the world, what she has done will also be told, in memory of her" (Matthew 26.13).

What do we learn from these Gospel stories? The woman presented herself before Jesus with her best offering. This does not require an explanation. Her attitude was the opposite of the host's (Luke). The host agreed to have Jesus in his house and sit with him at his table. However, he did not receive Jesus as expected. The lack of hospitality from the host was offered by a woman who was unexpected and questioned. Nonetheless, she looked past that and preferred to be at the feet of Jesus, who was at the table. Because of this gesture, she will be remembered in every place where the gospel is preached.

WORSHIPERS OF WIDTH

What do we learn about being worshipers of width through the Jenga game and the anointing of Jesus by a woman? Firstly, Jenga worship seeks height but lacks width, and it will not stand for long because any wind that comes will destroy it (Ephesians 4.14). This type of worship is not enduring. The moment will arrive when the pieces can no longer maintain the balance of the weight on top and fall. Another risk of those who develop a Jenga-type worship is that we are unable to see our faults, but we minimize the worship of others and question Jesus for receiving their worship. This is precisely what happens with Simon in Luke's version of the story. The attitude of Simon's heart was revealed because he did not care to develop the dimension of width. It is possible that, beyond pleasing Jesus, he was seeking personal benefit by having the Master in this house.

On the other hand, the woman displayed a distinct attitude. She did not have a house to receive guests, servants to follow her instructions, or friends to affirm her importance. She had only herself, an alabaster jar of perfume, and a desire to honor the presence of Jesus. As soon as she saw him, she threw herself at his feet. The story does not tell us why, but I dare say that she recognized what Simon could not. She recognized who was seated at the table. The true worshipers acknowledge that the presence of Jesus is primary. They take a posture of surrender, pour out their tears, wipe his feet, and anoint him with their best offering. That attitude is not only an expression of thanksgiving, but it also fills the house with the scent of perfume.

I want to confess that I do not know how many times I have come into the temple like Simon with a Jenga-type attitude of worship. But because of God's grace, someone comes to the feet of Jesus, and the breadth of their worship forces me to smell the fragrance of their perfume, which overcomes the strange smell with which I arrived.

Therefore, the question we need to ask ourselves is, how does our worship smell? Will it smell like the arrogance of the house's owner, or will it smell like the perfume of a strange woman who surrendered everything she had at the feet of Jesus?

Discussion questions:

1. In what ways can our worship impact the surrounding community?
2. How can we foster an inclusive worship environment that welcomes everyone?
3. Reflect on a time when someone else's worship experience impacted your own. What did you learn from that encounter?

LENGTH

the distance from the front portion
of the structure to the rear

FOUR

LENGTH

Philippians 3.12

In May 2016, I ran a half-marathon with my cousin Carlos. This was my first time signing up for a half-marathon. The longest distance I had run was 5K. Even though this would be my first time, I had an idea of what the preparation for this race would entail. My dad and brothers shared their experiences with me.

Carlos had experience in these types of races, so the first thing that he made me do was pay the registration fee. When I asked him why, his response was, "If you don't pay, you don't have a reason to prepare yourself. Once you put money on it, you won't want to lose it." Those words were so true! On many occasions, I thought about giving up, but then I thought about to the registration, and I encouraged myself to keep going.

My preparation lasted between three and four months. I created a weekly schedule where I ran at least four times a week. At first, it was easy because I had run those distances before. But as the distances extended, I began to feel the difficulty of running a half-marathon. As I continued to add miles, I noticed that the recovery time became shorter. The shorter distances from the first few weeks prepared me for the moments when I had to run for a longer time. What at first seemed insignificant ultimately helped me in the end. Moreover, as I kept extending my distance, I was able to enjoy a longer recovery period between runs. I longed for those moments of rest and recovery! It was these periods of rest when my body was oxygenated and relaxed.

During the preparation period, I maintained constant contact with Carlos. He was more experienced than I was, so I asked him questions to be prepared for race day. Carlos was very surprised by my dedication; what he did not know was that I did not want to let him down. He was the one with the experience, so I had to be prepared. I did not want to look bad!

Despite all the training and feedback from Carlos, nothing prepared me for the emotions I experienced during race day. I was not competing with anyone; I was not representing a team, yet I was extremely nervous. I think Carlos saw that I was a bit anxious. Hence, looked at me and said, "Wil, enjoy the moment, but don't let the emotions take control. If you let them lead, you are going to set a running pace that you won't be able to maintain, and you will not finish the race."

To make the long race short, I'll say that I ran a good race. I was physically and mentally prepared. As I ran, the emotions began to fall into place. It was an incredible experience. All the participants would encourage one another to keep going, whether walking or running at a slower pace. Additionally, the encouragement of the spectators and volunteers was a great help.

Two hours and seventeen minutes later, I was crossing the finish line with Carlos. We were tired, but when we saw our families and the finish line we had longed to reach, we kept going. Although I didn't see the finish line until the last half mile, I knew it was in front of me the whole time. I achieved the goal I set for myself, not that morning, but 4 months earlier when I decided to register. When I finished, I experienced an unforgettable sensation of satisfaction.

I WILL FOLLOW THE GOAL

Scripture compares the journey of the Christian life to a race a few times. One of the biblical authors who makes this comparison is Paul. In Philippians 3, we find an indirect example. In this chapter, Paul defends his total confidence in Christ. Paul does so to the point that he confesses that everything that he considers a gain is now a loss. "I consider everything a loss because of the surpassing worth of knowing Christ Jesus my Lord, for whose sake I have lost all things." (Philippians 3.8). Even though Paul could rest in everything he had accomplished in his life, he did not rest in these temporal things. He decided to put his total confidence in God, and for that reason, Paul knew that there was still so much to do.

This is where Paul connects our Christian journey with what might happen in a race. Paul knew that as long as there is life, a human being should strive for perfection. In verse 12, he says, "Not that I have already obtained all this, or have already arrived at my goal." Paul recognizes that, despite his maturity and intimate experience with the Lord, there is still a long way to go. Paul did not conform to the distance he had traveled and to his lived experiences. Even though he could not see everything clearly, there was a goal that needed to be reached. Therefore, he adds, "I do not consider myself yet to have taken hold of it" (Philippians 3.13). When we meditate on Paul's words, in the light of his testimony, we can find something important. When the Lord met with Paul on his way to Damascus, the Lord asked him, "Saul, Saul, why do you persecute (chase) me?" (Acts 9.4) During that first encounter, Paul, who at that time was named Saul, didn't pursue (follow) God, but he was persecuting him and his followers. Yet, after his conversion, as we read in his letter to the Philippians, we see that Paul is no longer persecuting God, but instead he is pursuing him.

When we persecute (chase) God, there is a self-motivation guiding us; we don't have a clear goal, and we make our own paths. But when we pursue (follow) God, we are not in charge of the journey, and God becomes our goal and path. When Paul chased God, he did it by human will and was motivated by earthly desires. But the Paul who is writing to this church, has heavenly motivations. He makes this clear when he states, "I press on toward the goal to win the prize for which God has called me heavenward in Christ Jesus." (Philippians 3.14).

Paul is convinced that a goal is in front of him. However, the goal is not his; God has made it possible through Jesus Christ. In other words, Paul did not set this goal. This goal is not a human one or an earthly one; it is divine. Because of this, Paul knows that as you continue to advance, you must push yourself in Christ Jesus. In this way, you can maintain a firm footing on this road that runs from the front to the back, expanding the dimension of length.

LET'S RUN WITH PATIENCE

The commitment to the Christian life requires dedication and effort. Few people will have a Christian life as short as the thief, to whom Jesus promises a life in paradise. It is for this reason that the last dimension is length. The invitation to be worshipers of length is like an invitation to a long-distance race. It is not an activity based on velocity but one of resistance,

PAUL WASN'T SATISFIED WITH THE DISTANCE HE'D TRAVELED OR THE EXPERIENCES HE'D LIVED. EVEN THOUGH HE COULDN'T SEE IT FROM WHERE HE STOOD, THERE WAS A FINISH LINE TO REACH.

dedication, endurance, and patience. The writer of the book of Hebrews describes it as such: "And let us run with perseverance the race marked out for us" (Hebrews 12.1). The author of Hebrews is inviting his readers to persevere in this race to eternal life. Paul's words to the church in Philippi are very similar. This heavenly goal does not compare to earthly goals. What is interesting and difficult about this is that this heavenly race is run on earth. The reality is that every day, we face difficulties and trials. This race, different from the one I ran, has many obstacles. Yet, Jesus told his disciples that "in this world you will have trouble" (John 16.33), but don't lose your trust. Despite the hurdles on our path, keep moving forward. Or, as the Hebrews states, get rid of "the sin that so easily entangles" (Hebrews 12.1). Like a runner should get rid of certain things before entering a race, a worshiper should get rid of the things that hinder their worship.

Previously, I mentioned that although we are running a race, neither the goal nor the race is ours. We have joined a race that has been run and completed. According to Hebrews chapter 12, Jesus is the one who initiates and completes the race. He, before us, suffered this race for "the joy set before him." On the other hand, there is a cloud of witnesses who went before us (Hebrews 11). All of them encourage us from heaven today, and their testimonies remind us that although this race is long, it demands perseverance. If we put our faith in Jesus, we can make it to the end.

Both Paul and the author of Hebrews have eternal life promised by the Father as their goal. But no one, according to the words of Jesus, knows the date and time of His return. The only clear thing is that we must keep ourselves in this race as we follow him. Those who die with hope, greet from afar the awaited goal, and those who kept their faith in His return, will rejoice with the goal they longed for. Until one or the other occurs, our responsibility is to maintain a life that is characterized by worship of length.

WORSHIPERS OF LENGTH

How do we achieve a lengthy and worshipful life? I propose some ideas that arise from the chapter itself. First, Carlos recommended registering for the event before I started training. This made me responsible for keeping up throughout the training season. Similarly, someone paid the price for us. Because of human disobedience, Adam and Eve removed themselves from the race too soon. They were unable to recognize what God had done in their favor. And they also did not recognize what God wanted to do through them. However, at the right moment, the Father sent his Son, born in the Spirit, to die for us so that we could again retake the race. We should not waste this opportunity.

One of the things I learned during training is that oxygenation plays a crucial role. When a person develops good oxygenation, they can improve their performance and reduce fatigue. This combination enables the runner to maintain pace in long-distance races. During the training, you gradually increase the distance and time. At the same time, you start adding resting time. This combination helps the body oxygenate and resist more during the race. On the other hand, during the race, there were moments when I had to listen to my body to know when I needed to drink water, eat some nutrients, or adjust my pace. These decisions, made in the middle of the race, helped me receive the necessary oxygen to continue. Similarly, the worshiper of length needs to grow daily. We must listen to what our body tells us, and occasionally, we need to slow down to replenish our spiritual nutrient levels. In the same way, just like there is an oasis at distinct points of the race, God tells us, "Come to me all who are weary and heavy laden, and I will give you rest" (Matthew 11.33). We renew our oxygenation resting in God daily. Only this way can we stay in the race.

Another important point is, don't run alone. This seems counterproductive because, on the day of the race, I was one among many people. However, having many people around you does not mean you are in good company. The best part of the race was being accompanied by Carlos. As I mentioned earlier, this was a great help. Moreover, I involved my family in this process. Even though Laura and our kids did not run, they encouraged me during the training, the race, and when I reached the finish line. However, there is another important aspect: when we arrived at the race venue, I noticed that other people were already there. Some had a lot of experience. Others were anxious like me. However, these interactions helped me realize that other people were willing to help and join us on our journey. Finally, some people did not run but served as volunteers during the race. They served us water, provided food, and offered words of encouragement. It was not only my race, but it was our race. In the same way, you and I are not the only worshipers in this journey. We are just one of many who have responded to this call. Some ran this race, and today they are part of the cloud of witnesses that encourages us to keep going. I do not know who your favorite character in the Bible is, but one of mine is Habakkuk. And in every moment that I feel my resistance failing, I think of Habakkuk encouraging me, "Wilmer, He will make your feet like the feet of a deer; you can do it" (Habakkuk 3.19). Don't run alone! We are not alone!

To close, let's remember that the goal is not ours. The goal belongs to God, and he has made Himself available to everyone who has decided to run this race. Furthermore, it is not our race; it's God's race. It doesn't matter how much you ran today; remember that tomorrow, we need to keep running. John said those who worship him will be measured. It won't be just me. In this race and finish line, there is room for many, and we are all invited to be worshippers of length. Let's press on!

Discussion questions:

1. How do you stay motivated in your spiritual journey when faced with challenges?
2. What does perseverance in worship look like in your life?
3. How can we support one another in running the race of faith together?

CONCLUSION

LET'S GROW

Ephesians 4.13

The Bible is full of examples that compare the life of a believer with organisms that, by nature, are dynamic and not static. For example, Psalm 1 affirms that we are "like a tree planted by streams of water" (Psalm 1.3). Even though the Psalmist presents an image of a tree already grown, we know that the tree goes through a growth process. Once a seed falls to the ground, it undergoes a process of growth that is like the tree that the Psalmist talks about. However, this seed cannot grow on its own; it requires assistance from several elements that provide it with essential nutrients. Firstly, it requires fertile soil. The minerals that are on the ground are crucial to this initial step. Secondly, it needs water. The water provides the humidity necessary for growth and helps distribute the minerals in the ground. Thirdly, it requires the sun. This supplies the necessary energy for the plant to make its food. And finally, oxygen. The oxygenation it receives on the surface reaches the roots and helps with the plant's growth. As we can see, even though it started as a small seed, the tree grew by being surrounded by basic elements. Not all trees grow at the same pace or to the same height, but they will grow, nonetheless.

CONTINUOUS GROWTH

This is the challenge I presented in this book: that we never stop growing. The Christian life is not static. On the contrary, the Christian life requires continuous growth. However, remember that, following the tree example, a forest is composed of many trees. Each one of them grows at its own pace and within its capacity. But altogether, they form a forest. So, grow, but do it at your own pace. We won't reach the same depth, height, width, or length yet; the most important thing is that we grow to our full potential.

No matter how much it scares us, let's look, let's follow, let's imitate, and let's grow like Jesus. He made Himself like us so that we could be like him. He is the best example of a worshiper in spirit and truth. Growing to the measure of Jesus is not impossible. If it were impossible, we would not have been invited to do so. I think that the difficulty is not being like Jesus. The difficulty lies in giving up what we have built ourselves. Leaving behind the idolatry of what we want to do is more difficult than living a life of worship in Jesus. Although summarizing the activity of Jesus in four points is a dangerous exercise, I will briefly present how the life of Jesus models a life of worship that is based on the four dimensions presented.

GROWING TO THE MEASURE OF CHRIST IS NOT IMPOSSIBLE. IF IT WERE IMPOSSIBLE, PAUL WOULDN'T HAVE INVITED US TO DO IT.

TO THE MEASUREMENT OF JESUS

Jesus modeled a life of *depth*. The depth is equal to firmness; it is the solid foundation of a building. Jesus built this foundation to develop an intimate relationship with the Father. The Gospels narrating the life of Jesus clearly describe that Jesus constantly looked to deepen his relationship with the Father. Luke affirms the following: "But Jesus often withdrew to lonely places and prayed" (Luke 5.16). Prayer, along with other spiritual disciplines that Jesus practiced, helped him solidify his relationship with the Father. This depth allowed Jesus to face the storms coming against him.

Jesus modeled a life of *height*. The height refers to our capacity to praise God with our lives. Jesus modeled height by recognizing that what he came to do was not his will but the Father's. In one of the most difficult moments of his life, Jesus understood that fulfilling the Father's will was necessary. Nearing the end of his life, while he prayed on the Mount of Olives, Jesus said to the Father, "My Father, if it is possible, may this cup be taken from me. Yet not as I will, but as you will" (Matthew 26.39). Worship that is defined by height does not rest in our desires; it rests in the will of him whom we worship. By obeying the will of the Father, Jesus returned to the place where it all started, seated at the right hand of the Father.

Jesus modeled a life of *width*. The width is the breadth of our worship. Jesus developed this dimension in his daily life. Wherever Jesus went, his testimony left a mark. A worshiper with a wide impact influences the lives of others through their own life. Mark describes it like this: "When Jesus had again crossed over by boat to the other side of the lake, a large crowd gathered around him while he was by the lake" (Mark 5.21). Wherever Jesus went, the people followed. His intimacy with the Father and his decision to fulfill the Father's will were a testimony to many. As soon as Jesus arrived, people would gather around him, and his presence would change the atmosphere of the place.

Jesus modeled a life of *length*. Length is the capacity to persevere. Jesus maintained this capacity to live a life dedicated to the Father. When he surrendered to the will of the Father, Jesus committed himself to a life of worship until the end. At the end of his life, John wrote that Jesus said, "It is finished." With that, he bowed his head and gave up his spirit." (John 19.30). Those who seek to be worshipers of length have to understand that this path requires commitment. This commitment was costly. This is why I previously mentioned that people often prefer to follow their desires rather than the will of the Father. However, Paul, who at one point lived following his desires, when he accepted the will of the Father, said this: "If we live, we live for the Lord; and if we die, we die for the Lord. So, whether we live or die, we belong to the Lord." (Romans 14.8). This is how I understand that Jesus modeled an identity of a worshiper that incarnates depth, height, width, and length.

Like the tree in the forest, you and I are not alone. We have been planted alongside other trees, and together, we form a big forest. Jesus, through the Father, sent us the Holy Spirit to help us grow in these four dimensions. The Spirit will reaffirm to us everything Jesus did. As a result, we will grow to the measurement of Jesus. On the other hand, in Jesus, our cornerstone, we are given the church, the community of faith; this is the perfect soil where we can receive the water, the light, and the continuous nourishment to take root, grow, mature, and give fruit.

Let's grow! Yes, but not to our measurement or the measurement of those around us. Our goal is to grow in the measurement of Jesus. These are the words of the apostle Paul to the church in Ephesus. If we live with this measurement as a guide, this will allow us to be part of the grand multitude that John saw in his vision. Thus, establish a relationship with the Father. Grown in the will of the Father. Impact with the testimony of the Father as you go. Persevere in your commitment to the Father until the end.

Discussion questions:

1. Reflecting on the dimensions of a worshiper, which area do you feel needs more attention in your life?
2. How can we as a group encourage continuous growth in each other's spiritual lives?
3. What practical steps can we take to ensure that our worship reflects the fullness of God's love and purpose?

www.ingramcontent.com/pod-product-compliance
Lightning Source LLC
Chambersburg PA
CBHW070640130626
46555CB00006B/2630